ISSUES today

A resource for KS3

Drugs

Editor: **Claire Owen**

ISSUE 24

Independence
Educational Publishers
Cambridge

First published by Independence
The Studio, High Green, Great Shelford
Cambridge CB22 5EG
England

© Independence 2009

British Library Cataloguing in Publication Data

Drugs – (Issues Today Series)
I. Owen, Claire II. Series
326.2'9

ISBN 978 1 86168 483 7

Acknowledgements

The publisher is grateful for permission to reproduce the following material.

While every care has been taken to trace and acknowledge copyright, the publisher tenders its apology for any accidental infringement or where copyright has proved untraceable. The publisher would be pleased to come to a suitable arrangement in any such case with the rightful owner.

Chapter One: Drug Abuse

Drugs in the UK, © Economic and Social Research Council, *Cannabis; Cocaine; Ecstasy; Solvents; Hallucinogens; Heroin; Speed,* © Crown copyright is reproduced with the permission of Her Majesty's Stationery Office, *Drug deaths*, DrugScope, *Young people and drug use*, © Crown copyright is reproduced with the permission of Her Majesty's Stationery Office, *Street drug trends*, © DrugScope, *Supply of cannabis*, © Joseph Rowntree Foundation.

Chapter Two: Tackling Drugs

New plan to tackle illegal drugs, © Crown copyright is reproduced with the permission of Her Majesty's Stationery Office, *Tackling substance misuse*, © Crown copyright is reproduced with the permission of Her Majesty's Stationery Office, *Drug legislation*, © Parents Against Drug Abuse, *Drugs and politics*, © politics.co.uk, *Q&A: cannabis reclassification*, © Guardian Newspapers Ltd, *Drug smuggling*, © Crown copyright is reproduced with the permission of Her Majesty's Stationery Office, *Should drugs be legalised?*, © Economics Essays.

All illustrations, including the cover, are by Don Hatcher.

Cover design, on behalf of Independence, by Hart McLeod Limited, Cambridge.

Printed in Great Britain by MWL Print Group Ltd.

Claire Owen
Cambridge
January, 2009

Issues today

Drugs

Contents

Chapter One: Drug Abuse

Chapter Two: Tackling Drugs

About Key Stage 3

Key Stage 3 refers to the first three years of secondary schooling, normally years 7, 8 and 9, during which pupils are aged between 11 and 14.

This series is also suitable for Scottish P7, S1 and S2 students.

About Issues Today

Issues Today is a series of resource books on contemporary social issues for Key Stage 3 pupils. It is based on the concept behind the popular *Issues* series for 14- to 18-year-olds, also published by Independence.

Each volume contains information from a variety of sources, including government reports and statistics, newspaper and magazine articles, surveys and polls, academic research and literature from charities and lobby groups. The information has been tailored to an 11 to 14 age group; it has been rewritten and presented in a simple, straightforward format to be accessible to Key Stage 3 pupils.

In addition, each *Issues Today* title features handy tasks and assignments based on the information contained in the book, for use in class, for homework or as a revision aid.

Issues Today can be used as a learning resource in a variety of Key Stage 3 subjects, including English, Science, History, Geography, PSHE, Citizenship, Sex and Relationships Education and Religious Education.

About this book

Drugs is the twenty-fourth volume in the *Issues Today* series. It looks at information about illegal drugs, trends in drug use and drugs and the law. Although the use of illegal drugs has fallen over the last ten years, it remains a serious problem for society. In 2007, 25% of pupils aged 11 to 15 said they had tried drugs at least once. What are the effects of illegal drugs and how is drug use being tackled?

Drugs offers a useful overview of the many issues involved in this topic. However, at the end of each article is a URL for the relevant organisation's website, which can be visited by pupils who want to carry out further research.

Because the information in this book is gathered from a number of different sources, pupils should think about the origin of the text and critically evaluate the information that is presented. Does the source have a particular bias or agenda? Are you being presented with facts or opinions? Do you agree with the writer?

At the end of each chapter there are two pages of activities relating to the articles and issues raised in that chapter. The 'Brainstorm' questions can be done as a group or individually after reading the articles. This should prompt some ideas and lead on to further activities. Some suggestions for such activities are given under the headings 'Oral', 'Moral Dilemmas', 'Research', 'Written' and 'Design' that follow the 'Brainstorm' questions.

For more information about *Issues Today* and its sister series, *Issues* (for pupils aged 14 to 18), please visit the Independence website.

www.independence.co.uk

Drugs in the UK

A DRUG IS A CHEMICAL SUBSTANCE that can change the way the mind and body works. Drugs can be natural or man-made and can be used for a variety of reasons. Alcohol, or drinks containing ethanol, have been consumed since pre-historic times and plants containing drugs have been chewed and smoked for thousands of years.

Medicinal drug use

Drugs are used widely for their healing or preventative properties. In the past, the benefits of natural drugs made from plants were passed down through generations and cultures and natural medicinal drugs are still widely used in many societies. Today the field of pharmacy is the application of chemical sciences for the use of medication. Pharmaceutical companies research, develop, market and supply healthcare drugs.

Recreational drug use

When a person's reason for using a drug is to get effects other than medical reasons it is known as recreational drug use. When an individual takes a drug occasionally rather than regularly, this is called casual use. The term implies that the user is not dependent or addicted.

Utilitarian drug use

Utilitarian drug use is when a person uses a drug for a particular benefit other than medical reasons or personal pleasure, such as helping them get to sleep or controlling their appetite. The lines between utilitarian use and abuse are hard to define and usually depend on the circumstance. Performance enhancing drugs taken by athletes would be considered drug abuse whereas amphetamines used to increase a soldiers endurance generally isn't thought of as drug abuse.

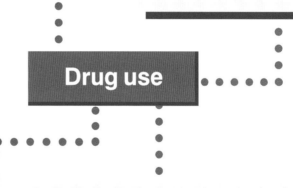

Drug abuse

The term drug abuse has different meanings in different situations.

▶ Some drugs, such as morphine, have medical purposes. If they are used for other reasons, or in unnecessarily large amounts, then the term 'drug abuse' is applied.

▶ Other substances, such as alcohol, are legal but do not serve a medical purpose. Using alcohol to a degree that is dangerous or damaging, either to the user or to others, is also understood as abuse.

▶ Any use of illegal substances that have no recognised medical purpose is generally regarded as abuse.

So the best general definition of drug abuse is the use of any drug in a way that does not follow medical advice or that does not follow a particular culture's accepted usage.

Drugs in the UK

The regulation and prohibition of drugs

The history of drug legislation in the UK and abroad is not one of simple health protection. Drugs such as alcohol and tobacco also have related health risks but are viewed as socially or culturally more acceptable than many other drugs.

In the UK, the main piece of legislation covering drugs is the Misuse of Drugs Act first introduced in 1971. The act groups drugs into various classifications, using an A, B and C grouping, where class A is considered the most harmful and therefore has the highest penalty.

Types of drugs

The effects of drugs vary greatly and can alter the way a person thinks, acts or feels along with many changes in a person's perception of the world around them. Drugs are usually placed into three broad categories based upon their effects:

Stimulants (Uppers)

Drugs that speed up or excite the central nervous system, and make you feel more alert, cause you to stay awake for long periods of time, reduce your appetite and make you feel good.

Examples – Cocaine/crack, amphetamines (speed), tobacco (nicotine), caffeine.

Depressants (Downers)

Drugs that slow down the central nervous system and make you less aware of the events around you.

Examples – Alcohol, opiates (painkillers), sedatives, tranquilisers.

Hallucinogens (Psychedelics)

Drugs that distort the senses and your awareness or perception of events. You might hallucinate - seeing or hearing things that don't actually exist.

Examples – LSD (acid), PCP, Ketamine, magic mushrooms.

Taking drugs

Drugs can be taken in various ways – including orally, by inhaling or by injection – and each is an important factor in the reaction to the drug. Many other factors can affect drug reactions, such as how much is taken, the setting and a person's tolerance to a drug. Tolerance to a drug develops when the response to the same dose of a drug decreases with repeated use.

Drug addiction

Addiction occurs when a person regularly takes a drug and finds it difficult to stop taking it. An addict may do almost anything to get hold of the drug. The dependency on a drug can be either physical or psychological. Withdrawal symptoms often occur when users stop taking a drug they have become physically dependent on.

www.esrcsocietytoday.ac.uk

The above information is reprinted with kind permission from the Economic and Social Research Council. © ESRC

Cannabis

CANNABIS IS THE MOST WIDELY USED illegal drug in Britain. Made from parts of the cannabis plant, it is a naturally occurring drug.

The effects

 Some people may feel chilled out, relaxed and happy, while others have one puff and feel sick. Others get the giggles and may become talkative.

 Hunger pangs are common and are known as 'getting the munchies'.

 Users may become more aware of their senses or get a feeling of slowing of time, which are due to its hallucinogenic effects.

 There is some psychological dependence with cannabis (where there is a desire to keep taking the drug even in spite of possible harms).

Appearance and use

Cannabis comes in different forms. Hash is a blacky-brown lump made from the resin of the plant. Grass or weed is made from the dried leaves of the plant and looks like tightly packed dried herbs.

Most people mix cannabis with tobacco and smoke it as a spliff or a joint. Some people put it in a pipe or bong, make tea with it or put it in food.

Slang

❝ Blow, dope, draw, ganja, grass, hash, hashish, hemp, herb, marijuana, pot, puff, resin, sinsemilla, skunk, smoke, spliff, wacky backy, weed. ❞

Class	C*
Estimated number of users (2007/08 British Crime Survey, Crown copyright)	2,382,000
Users as a % of the population (2007/08 British Crime Survey, Crown copyright)	7.4%
Average price per ounce (Street Drug Trends Survey 2008, Drugscope)	£89
Deaths involving cannabis in 2007 (Health Statistics Quarterly 39, ONS, Crown copyright)	12

* Cannabis will be reclassified as class B from January 2009.

The risks

▶ Smokers can become anxious, panicky and suspicious.

▶ Cannabis, like tobacco, has lots of chemical 'nasties', which can cause lung disease and cancer with long-term or heavy use, especially as it is often mixed with tobacco. It can also make asthma worse.

▶ Cannabis is risky for anyone with a heart problem as it increases the heart rate and can affect blood pressure.

▶ There's also increasing evidence of a link between cannabis and mental health problems such as schizophrenia. If you've a history of mental health problems or depression then taking this drug is not a good idea.

▶ Regular, heavy use makes it difficult to learn and concentrate. Some people begin to feel tired all the time and can't seem to get motivated.

www.talktofrank.com

The above information is reprinted with kind permission from FRANK. © Crown copyright

Cocaine

COCAINE POWDER, FREEBASE AND CRACK are all forms of cocaine. They are stimulants with powerful, but short-lived, effects. Stimulants temporarily speed up the processes of your mind and body.

The effects

- Taking cocaine makes users feel on top of the world. People taking it feel wide-awake, confident and on top of their game.

- Cocaine is a stimulant, so it can raise the body's temperature, make the heart beat faster and prevent feelings of hunger.

- Coke is very addictive. It can be difficult to resist the craving and strong psychological dependence due to changes in the brain.

Class	A
Estimated number of users *(2007/08 British Crime Survey, Crown copyright)*	740,000
Users as % of the population *(2007/08 British Crime Survey, Crown copyright)*	2.3%
Average price per gram *(Street Drug Trends Survey 2008, Drugscope)*	£42
Deaths involving any type of cocaine in 2007 *(Health Statistics Quarterly 39, ONS,* *Crown copyright)*	196

Slang

❝ *Coke, charlie, snow.* ❞

www.talktofrank.com

The above information is reprinted with kind permission from FRANK.
© Crown copyright

The risks

- ▶ Some people are over-confident on it and so may take careless risks.

- ▶ The hit from coke doesn't last long and from 'crack' lasts even less. When the effects start to wear off there can be a very strong temptation to take more.

- Crack and cocaine powder users have died from overdoses. High doses can raise the body's temperature, cause convulsions and respiratory or heart failure. Risk of overdosing increases if crack is mixed with heroin, sedatives or alcohol.

- Cocaine is highly risky for anybody with high blood pressure or a heart condition. Perfectly healthy, young people can have a fit or heart attack after taking too much coke and you may not know you've got a pre-existing heart condition.

- People who use crack or coke regularly often develop serious problems with anxiety and paranoia.

- Injecting any drug can cause vein damage and sharing needles and other injecting works can help the spread of HIV and hepatitis virus infections.

- Regularly smoking crack can cause breathing problems and damages the lungs.

Appearance and use

'Coke', or cocaine powder, is a white powder that's usually snorted up the nose.

'Crack' is a form of cocaine made into small lumps or rocks (which makes a cracking noise when burnt). It's usually smoked in a pipe, glass tube, plastic bottle or in foil.

Both powder and crack forms of cocaine can be prepared to make a solution for injecting.

Mini glossary

convulsions – *an uncontrollable fit in which the body starts jerking violently*

respiratory failure – *condition which affects breathing or the lungs*

Ecstasy

IN THE EARLY 90s clubbers started taking Ecstasy to stay awake and dance for hours. The effects take about half an hour to kick in and tend to last between 3 to 6 hours, followed by a gradual comedown.

The effects

An E gives people an energy buzz that makes them feel alert and alive.

Ecstasy makes people feel in tune with their surroundings – sounds and colours are more intense.

Users often feel great love for the people they're with and the strangers around them. Lots of people feel chatty on E.

Class	A
Estimated number of users *(2007/08 British Crime Survey, Crown copyright)*	470,000
Users as a % of the population *(2007/08 British Crime Survey, Crown copyright)*	1.5%
Average price per pill *(Street Drug Trends Survey 2008, Drugscope)*	£2.30
Deaths involving ecstasy in 2007 *(Health Statistics Quarterly 39, ONS, Crown copyright)*	47

Appearance and use

Usually in tablet form, Es come in all sorts of colours and some of them have pictures or logos stamped into them. They are usually swallowed although some people do smoke or snort them. Pure Ecstasy is a white crystalline powder known as MDMA.

The risks

▶ Physical side effects can develop that include: dilated pupils, a tingling feeling, tightening of the jaw muscles, raised body temperature and the heart beats faster.

▶ Short-term effects of use can include anxiety, panic attacks, confused episodes and paranoid or psychotic states.

▶ There's no way of telling what's in an E until you've swallowed it. So, there may be negative side effects from other ingredients in the tablet.

▶ There have been over 200 ecstasy-related deaths in the UK since 1996. Ecstasy use is the cause of death in many of the cases but there have been some involving other substances sold as Ecstasy.

▶ Ecstasy affects the body's temperature control. Dancing for long periods in a hot atmosphere increases the chances of overheating and dehydration. Take regular breaks from the dance floor to cool down.

▶ Be careful with fluids though, as drinking too much can also be dangerous or even fatal. Ecstasy can cause the body to release a hormone which prevents the production of urine. Drink too quickly and it interferes with your body's salt balance, which can be as deadly as not drinking enough water. Reduce the risks by sipping no more than a pint of water or non-alcoholic fluid every hour.

▶ Anyone with a heart condition, blood pressure problems, epilepsy or asthma can have a very dangerous reaction to the drug.

Slang

❝ *E, pills, brownies, Mitsubishis, Rolexes, Dolphins, XTC.* ❞

www.talktofrank.com

The above information is reprinted with kind permission from FRANK.
© Crown copyright

Solvents

SOLVENTS COVER A HUGE NUMBER OF SUBSTANCES: gas lighter refills, aerosols containing hairspray, deodorants and air fresheners, tins or tubes of glue, some paints, thinners and correcting fluids, cleaning fluids, surgical spirit, dry-cleaning fluids and petroleum products.

The effects

⊘ Users say it's like being drunk with dizziness, dreaminess and fits of the giggles. And it can be difficult to think straight.

⊘ Depending on what's being inhaled, you can hallucinate. This can last for up to 45 minutes.

⊘ It can give people a 'hangover' afterwards, giving them severe headaches and leaving them tired.

The risks

▶ People can experience vomiting and blackouts.

▶ There's a risk of fatal heart problems which have been known to kill users the very first time they sniff.

▶ Squirting gas products down the throat is a particularly dangerous way of taking the drug. It can make your throat swell so you can't breathe and slows down your heart.

▶ You risk suffocation if you inhale from a plastic bag over your head.

▶ Sniffing can seriously affect your judgement and when you're high there's a real danger you'll try something reckless.

▶ Long-term abuse of solvents has been shown to damage the brain, liver and kidneys.

▶ It can be hard to get the amount right. Just enough will give the desired high – a little too much can result in coma.

The law

Solvent misuse isn't illegal, but it is illegal in England and Wales for shopkeepers to sell you intoxicating substances if they think you're likely to be inhaling them. In Scotland the law is different but the effect is similar. Under Scottish law you can be prosecuted for 'recklessly' selling substances to any age group if you suspect they're going to inhale them.

Since October 1999, the law makes it an offence to supply gas lighter refills to anyone under the age of 18. This law applies to the whole of the UK.

www.talktofrank.com

Appearance and use

All households have different substances which, when abused, can cause different effects.

Solvents are sniffed from a cloth, a sleeve or a plastic bag. Some users put a plastic bag over their heads and inhale that way. Gas products can be squirted directly into the back of the throat which makes it difficult to control the dose.

DID YOU KNOW?

According to the latest British Crime Survey figures, around one in three 16- to 59-year-olds have ever used illicit drugs.

Drug Misuse Declared: Findings from the 2007/08 British Crime Survey. October 2008 © Crown copyright

Hallucinogens

HALLUCINOGENIC DRUGS DISTORT your senses and the way you view objects and reality, sometimes in the form of hallucinations.

The effects

- The experience is known as a 'trip' and these trips can be good or bad. Once it's started you can't stop it.

- A 'trip' can appear to involve a speeding up and slowing down of time and movement.

- Colour, sound and objects can get distorted and you can experience double vision.

Magic mushrooms

Class	A
Estimated number of users *(2007/08 British Crime Survey, Crown copyright)*	156,000
Users as a % of the population *(2007/08 British Crime Survey, Crown copyright)*	0.5%
Average price per ounce, dried *('Drugs - facing facts', RSA Commission on Illegal Drugs, Communities and Public Policy)*	£6

Magic mushrooms are mushrooms that grow in the wild. The most common form is a species called psilocybe semilanceata or 'liberty cap', which are small and tan-coloured and bruise blue when they're touched. The stronger variety is amanita muscaria or 'fly agaric', which are more like the red and white spotted toadstools you see in fairytale books. After picking, mushrooms are often eaten raw or are dried out and stored.

Slang

66 *Liberties, magics, mushies, liberty cap, shrooms, Amani, agaric.* 99

www.talktofrank.com

The risks

- ▶ 'Bad trips' are seriously frightening and unsettling. And you can't tell whether you're going to have a bad trip or a good trip.

- ▶ Flashbacks sometimes happen. This is when part of the trip is later re-lived after the original experience.

- ▶ You may be at risk when you're not in complete control of what you're doing. Your perception of your body and the world around you can be distorted.

- ▶ LSD and magic mushrooms can complicate any mental health issues you may have.

- ▶ Mushrooms can make you feel sick, tired and disoriented. Eating the wrong kind of mushroom can make you seriously ill and even kill you.

LSD

Class	A
Estimated number of users *(2007/08 British Crime Survey, Crown copyright)*	88,000
Users as a % of the population *(2007/08 British Crime Survey, Crown copyright)*	0.3%
Average price per tab *('Drugs - facing facts', RSA Commission on Illegal Drugs, Communities and Public Policy)*	£1-5

LSD or Lysergic Acid Diethylamide originally comes from ergot, a fungus found growing wild on rye and other grasses.

LSD is usually sold as tiny squares of paper with pictures on them, but it can be found as a liquid or as tiny pellets. It can be sucked or swallowed.

Slang

66 *Acid, blotter, cheer, dots, drop, flash, hawk, L, lightening flash, liquid acid, Lucy, micro dot, stars, tab.* 99

Heroin

HEROIN IS A NATURAL OPIATE made from morphine (opiates dull pain).

The effects

▶ Heroin slows down body functioning and reduces physical and psychological pain.

▶ A small dose of heroin gives the user a feeling of warmth and well-being.

▶ Bigger doses can make the user sleepy and very relaxed.

▶ The first dose of heroin can bring about dizziness and vomiting.

▶ Heroin is highly addictive.

Appearance and use

Brownish white powder. It can either be smoked, injected or snorted.

The risks

▶ Overdoses can lead to coma and even death from respiratory failure (i.e. when breathing stops).

▶ There's also a risk of death due to inhaling vomit as heroin stops the body's cough reflex working properly.

▶ Injecting heroin can damage your veins and has been known to lead to gangrene (death and decay of body tissue, usually a finger, toe or limb) and tissue infections.

▶ Sharing needles and other works to inject puts you in danger of infections like hepatitis B or C and HIV/AIDS.

Class	A
Estimated number of users *(2007/08 British Crime Survey, Crown copyright)*	34,000
Users as a percentage of population *(2007/08 British Crime Survey, Crown copyright)*	0.1%
Average price per gram *(Street Drug Trends Survey 2008, Drugscope)*	£49
Deaths involving heroin and morphine in 2007 *(Health Statistics Quarterly 39, ONS, Crown copyright)*	829

Speed

'SPEED' IS THE STREET NAME for a range of amphetamines. Amphetamines are stimulants that people take to keep them awake and alert.

The effects

• Speed makes people feel wide awake, excited and chatty.

• You can get strongly addicted to amphetamines.

Class	B*
Estimated number of users *(2007/08 British Crime Survey, Crown copyright)*	329,000
Users as a % of the population *(2007/08 British Crime Survey, Crown copyright)*	1.0%
Average price per gram *(Street Drug Trends Survey 2008, Drugscope)*	£9
Deaths involving amphetamines in 2007, excluding ecstasy and MDMA *(Health Statistics Quarterly 39, ONS , Crown copyright)*	50

*Prepared-for-injection Speed is Class A.

The risks

▶ Speed can make it difficult to relax or sleep.

▶ Speed users have died from overdoses.

▶ Speed puts a strain on your heart. It's not advisable for people with high blood pressure or a heart condition.

▶ Speed can lead to anxiety, depression, irritability and aggression as well as mental illness such as psychosis.

Appearance and use

Off-white or pinkish powder or white pills. It is dabbed onto the gums, snorted, swallowed, mixed in drinks or injected.

www.talktofrank.com

The above information is reprinted with kind permission from FRANK.
© Crown copyright

Drug deaths

HOW MANY PEOPLE DIE from drugs? The straight answer is that we do not know exactly how many drug-related deaths there are in the UK.

This is because:

1 There is no one organisation that collects information about drug-related deaths, for all of the UK.

2 There is no one definition of what we mean by drug-related deaths. For example, it could include:

▶ people who are dependent on drugs and overdose

▶ suicides by overdose of people who have no previous history of using drugs

▶ accidental poisoning or overdose

▶ ecstasy related deaths where people have died from overheating through dancing non-stop in hot clubs rather than from the direct effect of the drugs

▶ deaths associated with cigarette smoking

▶ deaths from accidents where people are drunk or under the influence of drugs

▶ murders and manslaughters where people are drunk or under the influence of drugs

▶ deaths from driving while drunk or intoxicated

▶ deaths from AIDS among injecting drug users

▶ deaths which had nothing to do with the presence of a drug in the body.

3 Cause of death is recorded on death certificates but doctors may not mention drugs, even where drugs might be involved.

Mini glossary

manslaughter – causing the death of a person without planning or intending to

intoxicated – under the influence of a chemical substance

Despite these difficulties there are estimates of the possible number of deaths associated with different drugs:

Tobacco

It is estimated that each year in the UK around 114,000 people die from tobacco-related diseases.

Alcohol

Estimates of annual alcohol-related deaths in England and Wales vary from 5,000 to 40,000.

Solvents

47 deaths associated with volatile substance abuse were recorded in 2004.

Ecstasy

Deaths associated with different illegal drugs are also difficult to judge accurately. One exception is ecstasy with over 250 ecstasy-related deaths being reported between 1999 and 2004.

AIDS

Deaths from AIDS among injecting drug users who have contracted HIV by sharing injecting equipment are also difficult to judge exactly. However, by December 2004 over 4,200 drug injectors had tested positive for HIV in the UK. Of that total over 1,200 [29%] had been diagnosed with full-blown AIDS and 1545 had died.

In relation to the whole range of problems which can happen to those who use drugs, death is by far the least likely outcome, but one which, not surprisingly, attracts most attention and causes most concern. Like all data about illegal drug use, information about deaths comes from a variety of sources that combine to present a patchy and incomplete picture. For this reason this is a highly simplified overview of what we know about deaths from drug use and how these compare to deaths caused by alcohol and tobacco.

www.drugscope.org.uk

Young people and drug use

THE PREVALENCE OF DRUG USE HAS DECLINED overall since 2001. In 2007, 25% of pupils said they had tried drugs at least once, down from 29% in 2001. There were falls over the same period in the number of pupils who said they had taken drugs in the last year and the last month. The decline in the prevalence of drug use reflects a fall in the proportions of pupils who have ever been offered drugs over a similar period, from 42% to 36%.

How many young people take drugs?

In 2007, 17% of pupils said they had taken drugs in the last year and 10% in the last month. The prevalence of drug use is similar among boys and girls, and increases with age. 6% of 11-year-olds had taken drugs in the last year; at the age of 15, 31% of pupils had taken drugs in the last year.

How often do young people take drugs?

Most pupils who take drugs do not do so often. A third (34%) of pupils who had taken drugs in the last year said they usually take drugs once a month or more, only 5% of pupils overall. Among those who had taken drugs in the last year, 28% said they had only ever taken drugs once, and a further 31% had taken drugs on five or fewer occasions.

Which drugs do young people take?

As in previous years, pupils are more likely to take cannabis than any other drug:

▶ in 2007, 9% of pupils reported taking cannabis within the last year;

▶ sniffing glue, gas, aerosols or solvents is the next most common form of drug use (6% of pupils in the last year);

▶ followed by sniffing poppers (5%).

The use of other drugs by this age group is rare. Overall, 4% of pupils report having taken one of the eight Class A drugs asked about, though no single Class A drug had been taken by more than 2% of pupils in the last year.

Two-fifths of pupils (39%) who took drugs in the last year took more than one type of drug.

Young people and drug use

Why do young people try drugs?

The most common reason for trying drugs is 'to see what it was like' (55%); relatively few pupils try drugs to get high or feel good (18%) or because their friends are taking drugs (17%). The first experience of drug taking is equally likely to leave the pupil feeling good (43%) or no different (44%).

Pupils' first drug use is more likely to be sniffing volatile substances than any other type of drug.

Nearly three-quarters (72%) of pupils get their first drugs from friends.

Hazardous behaviours

Drug taking is associated with other hazardous behaviours; the odds of having taken drugs in the last year and in the last month increase with the frequency of smoking and the amount of alcohol drunk in the last week.

Pupils who have been excluded from school or who have played truant also have a greater likelihood of having taken drugs.

Attitudes towards drugs

Pupils tend to feel that drug use is not acceptable behaviour within their age group:

▶ A minority think that it is OK for someone of their age to try cannabis once (10%);

▶ 9% think it is OK to try sniffing glue;

▶ 3% think it is OK to try cocaine.

They are even less likely to be sympathetic to regular drug use:

▶ 6% think it is OK for someone of their age to take cannabis once a week;

▶ 4% think it is OK to sniff glue once a week;

▶ 2% think it is OK to take cocaine once a week.

Attitudes change with age, in line with the prevalence of drug use; for example, 13% of 15-year-olds think that it is OK for someone of their age to take cannabis once a week, compared with 1% of 11-year-olds.

Pupils also tend to feel that their parents would (or do) disapprove strongly of drug taking:

▶ Most (86%) think their families would try to stop them taking drugs;

▶ 13% think their families would try to persuade them to stop;

▶ 1% think their families would do nothing;

▶ less than 1% think their families would encourage them.

www.ic.nhs.uk

Mini glossary

prevalence – *widespread occurrence*

hazardous – *risky or dangerous*

played truant – *missed school without permission*

This survey is the latest in a series designed to monitor smoking, drinking and drug use among secondary school pupils aged 11 to 15. Information was obtained from 7,831 pupils in 279 schools throughout England in the autumn of 2007.

17 July 2008

The above information is an extract from the report 'Drug use, smoking and drinking among young people in England in 2007' and is reprinted with kind permission from the NHS Information Centre. © Crown copyright

Street drug trends

THE KEY TREND IDENTIFIED by the annual Street Drug Trends Survey from DrugScope is a rise in the use of the tranquiliser diazepam, primarily among heroin and crack cocaine users.

The class C drug, better known as Valium, has been on the illicit market in the UK for some years but 15 out of 20 locations reported rising levels of diazepam use among class A drug users over the past 12 months. Diazepam is being used as a heroin substitute and is often taken alongside alcohol and methadone to ease the comedown from crack cocaine, a potentially lethal combination. There was some evidence that diazepam was also being used by problem drinkers, powder cocaine users and among some young people.

Martin Barnes, chief executive of DrugScope, commenting on the survey findings said:

66 The rise in the use of illicitly imported diazepam is concerning particularly as drug users face a high risk of overdose when using the drug in combination with other drugs such as methadone and alcohol.

'The fact that the survey identified some evidence of increasing diazepam use among young people is also worrying. We know from last year's research that some young people are combining use of alcohol, cocaine, cannabis and ecstasy. The addition of diazepam increases risk, including where the drug is mixed with alcohol. 99

www.drugscope.org.uk

The above information is reprinted with kind permission from DrugScope.
© DrugScope

Other drug trends

- National average street drug prices have remained relatively stable over the past 12 months, with only minor changes in price.

- Polydrug use – using combinations of alcohol, cannabis, cocaine and ecstasy – was highlighted by several respondents as a significant problem among some young people.

- Commercially home-grown skunk cannabis was dominating the cannabis market in many areas, with users finding it hard to get hold of lower strength resin or imported herbal cannabis.

- The key trend identified in last year's survey, the development of a 'two tier' cocaine market, was still noticeable, with dealers selling low quality powder for an average of £30 per gram and higher quality for £50. Across most towns and cities surveyed cocaine continues to be a popular drug.

- In the ecstasy market, there was an increase in the amphetamine-like drug BZP, better known as being sold as a 'legal high', replacing MDMA as the ingredient in pills.

3 September 2008

Mini glossary

tranquiliser – *a drug used to reduce stress*

diazepam – *medication for anxiety, which is only legally available on prescription*

comedown – *the after effects of drug use, which can include depression and anxiety*

lethal – *can cause death*

two tier – *two levels*

Supply of cannabis

CANNABIS SUPPLY TO YOUNG PEOPLE is largely through social networks and friendship groups rather than through overtly criminal drug markets. This is according to a new study from the Institute for Criminal Policy Research published by the Joseph Rowntree Foundation.

Just over 2.5 million young people (16-24) in England and Wales have used cannabis with an average starting age of 14. Yet how young people access and use the drug has rarely been considered in the UK. Not enough research has been conducted into how the criminal justice or education systems deal with young people caught supplying or brokering cannabis – helping others access the drug but not for profit.

66 *Nearly all of the 182 young cannabis users interviewed were introduced to the drug by friends.* 99

The report – *Cannabis Supply and Young People: 'It's a social thing'* – provides a snapshot of how young people in a large city and rural villages get hold of cannabis. Researchers found that nearly all of the 182 young cannabis users interviewed were introduced to the drug by friends; used the drug with friends; and accessed the drug through friends. Only 6% had bought the drug from an unknown seller so most of them were distanced from overtly criminal drug markets.

Findings

▶ Nearly all interviewees reported cannabis to be 'very easy' or 'fairly easy' to buy.

▶ Over three-quarters stated that they could get cannabis in less than an hour.

▶ 'Chipping in' and sharing cannabis with friends to make it more affordable was a common way of buying the drug for 70% of those interviewed.

▶ Most of the young people were aware that they would be arrested if they were caught selling cannabis.

▶ Amongst those interviewed, 45% had either sold cannabis or brokered access to the drug without making a profit – nearly always to friends and acquaintances. They did not generally see themselves as dealers although they acknowledged that they could be seen as such by others and by the criminal justice system.

Professor Mike Hough, Director of the Institute of Criminal Policy Research said:

66 While the public stereotype of the drug dealer may be of an adult stranger 'pushing' drugs to young people, in the case of cannabis, this is very rarely the case. Most young people get their cannabis from other young people – often without a profit being made. 99

31 January 2008

Mini glossary

overtly – *openly*

brokering – *negotiating*

profit – *money gained*

stereotype – *fixed idea of a person or group*

www.jrf.org.uk

The above information is adapted from a press release with kind permission from the Joseph Rowntree Foundation. © Joseph Rowntree Foundation

Activities

Brainstorm

Brainstorm to find out what you know about drugs.

1. What are drugs?

   ....

   ....

2. What is drug abuse?

   ....

   ....

3. What are the three types of drugs?

   ....

   ....

   ....

Oral activities

4. Why do you think young people might decide to try drugs? Discuss in a group.

   NOTES ....

   ....

   ....

5. Do you think celebrities glamorise drug taking? Discuss with a partner.

   NOTES ....

   ....

   ....

Moral Dilemmas

6. Some of your friends want to take drugs and try to persuade you to join in. What do you do?

7. You have found out that one of your classmates is supplying drugs to other pupils at your school. You are worried as some of your friends are talking about trying drugs and have asked the classmate to get hold of some for them. What do you do? Who could you talk to about your concerns?

Activities

Research activities

8. Taking drugs can have serious effects on your mental health as well as your physical health. Research a mental health problem that may be triggered or worsened by taking drugs and summarise your findings for the rest of the class.

   NOTES..

   ....

   ....

   ....

   ....

9. Visit the FRANK website at www.talktofrank.com. How helpful do you think this website is for young people looking for information on drugs? Do you think the site is appealing to young people?

   ....

   ....

   ....

   ....

   ....

Written activities

Complete the following activities in your exercise books or on a sheet of paper.

10. Choose one of the drugs mentioned in Chapter One, such as cannabis or cocaine, and write an informative leaflet for young people highlighting the potential dangers of taking this drug.

11. Write a letter to an 'agony aunt' from a young person with a drug problem and then write a response back to them offering support and suggestions of where they can get help.

Design activities

12. Draw a diagram of the human body and show how drugs can affect various parts of the body, such as the brain, nervous system and lungs.

New plan to tackle illegal drugs

THE GOVERNMENT'S NEW ten-year strategy for fighting illegal drugs is designed to ensure that fewer young people ever use drugs, and that those who do use drugs get help to kick the habit and re-establish their lives. It aims to cut drug-related crime, and to reduce the damage that drugs do in our communities.

Drug use at 11-year low

Over the last decade, use of illegal drugs in the UK has fallen to an 11-year low. Drug-related crime has dropped by a fifth over the last five years.

Investment in drug treatment has more than doubled the number of people getting treatment – 195,000 in the last year.

Compulsory drug testing of people who have been arrested, backed up by tough punishment – including prison sentences – has contributed to a fall in recorded theft and robbery.

But tackling drugs remains a huge social problem. Use of Class A drugs costs the UK £15 billion a year in crime and health costs alone.

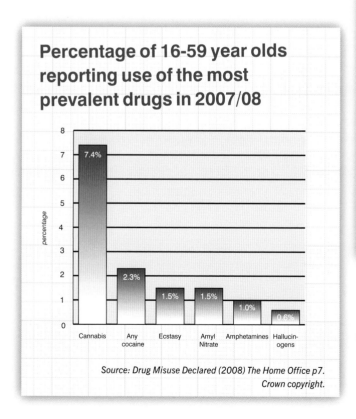

Percentage of 16-59 year olds reporting use of the most prevalent drugs in 2007/08

Source: Drug Misuse Declared (2008) The Home Office p7. Crown copyright.

Investment

This year the government will invest almost £1 billion in the programmes behind the new strategy. This investment will help to:

▶ extend police powers to seize drug dealers' assets, ensuring that crime doesn't pay;

▶ place more responsibility on drug-users on benefits to get treatment and jobs;

▶ tackle drugs through neighbourhood policing;

▶ strengthen and extend international agreements to stop drugs before they reach the UK;

▶ focus on families where parents use drugs; and prioritising treatment for parents in order to protect children;

▶ try new approaches that allow more flexible use of resources, and more personalised treatment;

▶ increase the use of community sentences, including some that require drug rehabilitation;

▶ develop support for drug treatment, so that those who quit drugs get training and support so they can get back to work, and re-establishing their lives.

Over the last decade, use of illegal drugs in the UK has fallen to an 11-year low.

New plan to tackle illegal drugs

Use of illegal drugs 'destroys families'

Home Secretary Jacqui Smith said the strategy well help to reach the government's goal of ensuring that fewer people use drugs.

'Illegal drug use is unacceptable. It wastes lives, destroys families and damages communities,' she said. 'We want those who do use drugs to enter and finish treatment, and move on to lead healthy, drug-free lives.'

She said the government plans to continue to send a clear message that it is on the side of communities.

'We demand respect for the law, and we will not tolerate illegal or anti-social behaviour. But we will provide help for those who are trying to turn their lives around, to get off drugs and into work. However, we expect drug users themselves to take responsibility, and we will help them to do so.'

Tailored approach

Among other things, the government will change the rules of the benefits system in order to provide a more personalised approach. This will ensure that drug users receive support fitted to their needs.

In return, they will be required to attend drug treatment sessions.

Health Secretary Alan Johnson pointed out that gains have already been made in terms of treatment, and over the past ten years treatment options have grown. More people are getting treatment and they're waiting less time for help.

'Every drug user is different,' he said. 'This strategy ensures that treatment is personalised to suit individual needs. A key element is an innovative new pilot scheme which will help drug users who are on benefits get into treatment, get a job and live a drug-free life.'

Faster treatment for families with drug problems

Children, Schools and Families Secretary Ed Balls said only a small number of parents are drug-users, but even a small number is too many as the situation puts children at risk.

Because of that concern, the new strategy ensures that parents with dependent children will get better and faster access to specialist drug treatment.

'At the heart of the new drugs strategy is recognising the influence of families in tackling the problem,' he said. 'So we will help parents by providing more information and support to help them talk to their children about drugs.'

27 February 2008

Mini glossary

compulsory – *required*

invest – *put money into*

assets – *valuable possessions, such as property*

prioritising – *putting first*

rehabilitation – *treatment to help overcome drug dependency*

innovative – *progressive*

pilot scheme – *a trial of a policy to test how effective it is*

dependent – *reliant on another person*

http://drugs.homeoffice.gov.uk

Tackling substance misuse

For every £1 spent on drug treatment there is a saving of £9.50 to society as a whole.

96% of drug users are receiving treatment within three weeks of being assessed.

The Government is investing £604 million in drug treatment in 2008/09.

Drug related deaths have fallen by 13% since 2001 following sharp increases in the 1990's.

£54.3 million of new funding is being invested to increase inpatient detoxification and residential rehabilitation services.

Drug related crime has reduced by 20% since 2003 among those individuals referred for drug treatment through the Criminal Justice System.

195,000 people received treatment in 2006/7, 130% more than in 1998.

83% of young people are aware of FRANK, the government's drugs awareness campaign. The number of 15-18 year olds agreeing that smoking cannabis damages the mind went up from 45% to 61% as a result of this campaign.

Three out of four people stay in treatment for at least 12 weeks. (Staying in treatment for 12 weeks has a lasting positive impact and is a measure of successful treatment).

9 July 2008

DID YOU KNOW? *Use of any illicit drug in the last year has decreased from 11.1 per cent in 1996 to 9.3 per cent in 2007/08, partly because of declines in the use of cannabis.*

Drug Misuse Declared: Findings from the 2007/08 British Crime Survey. October 2008 © Crown copyright

www.dh.gov.uk

The above information is reprinted with kind permission from the Department of Health. © Crown copyright

Drug legislation

Misuse of Drugs Act 1971

Controls the unauthorised use of drugs considered capable of 'having harmful effects sufficient to constitute a social problem.' Also defines the offences relating to producing, growing, supplying and possessing certain drugs.

Medicines Act 1968

Governs the manufacture and supply of medicines, some of which are also controlled by the Misuse of Drugs Act.

Customs & Excise Management Act 1979

Penalises unauthorised import and export of illegal drugs.

Drug Trafficking Act 1986

Makes it an offence to sell articles for the administration or preparation of illegal drugs, and allows for the seizure of assets related to money from drug trafficking.

Road Traffic Act 1972

Makes it an offence to be in charge of a motor vehicle whilst unfit to drive through drink or drugs (including solvents).

Summary of the main UK drug-related legislation

Controlled Drugs (Penalties) Act 1985

Increased the maximum penalties for trafficking in Class 'A' drugs.

The Health & Safety at Work Act 1974

Requires that employers ensure, as far as it is reasonably practicable, the health, safety and welfare at work of their employees. It is possible that in certain circumstances charges may be brought against an employer who knowingly allows a drug abuser to continue working without doing anything either to help the abuser or to protect the rest of the workforce.

Intoxicating Substances (Supply) Act 1985

Controls sales and supply of solvents to under 18s in the UK.

Mini glossary

sufficient – enough

constitute – to make up

import – bring goods in from a foreign country

export – send goods abroad

www.pada.org.uk

The above information is reprinted with kind permission from Parents Against Drug Abuse. © PADA

Drugs and politics

What are drugs?

Drugs include a broad range of substances ranging from prescription medicines, to illegal street drugs such as cocaine and ecstasy, to readily available products such as tobacco and alcohol.

In public health and political terms, 'drugs' usually refers to recreational drugs, specifically those which are illegal under the Misuse of Drug Act. Although technically a mind-altering substance, alcohol is not commonly included in the drugs debate, with binge drinking treated as a separate issue. Similarly, tobacco calls for its own debate.

Background

The UK government has taken a prohibitive stance towards recreational drugs, which is enforced through the Misuse of Drugs Act 1971.

This makes it an offence to possess drugs for personal use or with the intention to supply them to others, or to allow buildings you occupy or manage to be used for drug taking. It does not make it a specific offence to be under the influence of controlled substances.

The act created the Advisory Council on the Misuse of Drugs, which became responsible for distinguishing three separate classes of controlled substances, referred to as Class A, Class B and Class C drugs. This classification system both attempts to rank the harm caused by various drugs and set appropriate penalties for their use.

When assessing the classification of new drugs, the Advisory Council on the Misuse of Drugs hears evidence from law enforcement agencies, charities, professional bodies and scientific evidence. It classifies drugs using a risk assessment template, which looks at physical harm, dependence and social harms.

Drugs policy

Drugs policy in the UK is the responsibility of the Home Office. This makes it a criminal matter and yet many argue drugs policy would be better overseen by the Department of Health. Similarly, the ABC drugs classification system has been criticised for combining physical and social harm caused with criminal penalties.

The UK adopts a policy of prohibition towards drugs. Some people argue that drugs policy should move from abstinence education and government attempts to disrupt supply to focus on harm reduction policies.

It has also been argued that criminalising all drugs creates a criminal group to meet the demand for recreational substances. This in turn has been linked to other forms of crimes including gang violence. However, calls to legalise all drugs are politically unpopular and the late Mo Mowlam is one of the few members of the political establishment to have made the case for legalising all hard drugs.

Penalties for possession and supply of drugs

Class	Penalty for possession	Penalty for supply	Includes
Class A	Up to seven years in prison or an unlimited fine or both.	Up to life in prison or an unlimited fine or both.	Ecstasy, heroin, LSD, cocaine, crack, magic mushrooms and amphetamines (if injected).
Class B	Up to five years in prison or an unlimited fine or both.	Up to 14 years in prison or an unlimited fine or both.	Amphetamines, Ritalin, pholcodine and cannabis (from January 2009).
Class C	Up to two years in prison or an unlimited fine or both.	Up to 14 years in prison or an unlimited fine or both.	Cannabis (until January 2009, when cannabis is reclassified Class B), tranquilisers, some painkillers, GHB and ketamine.

Drugs and politics

The ABC system

Many sources have accused the ABC system of inconsistency, noting that the criminal penalties given to various drugs do not always equate to the harm caused.

A study published in the Lancet in spring 2007 concluded UK drug's policy was not fit for purpose. Looking at the harm caused by various drugs, it found alcohol was the fifth most dangerous drug available, following heroin, cocaine, barbiturates and methadone, yet it is not included in the ABC system. Tobacco came out as the ninth most dangerous drug, ahead of cannabis and the Class A drugs ecstasy and LSD.

In October 2007, police constable Richard Brunstrom said:

66 The current classification of controlled drugs has no sound underpinning logic. Most importantly the ABC system illogically excludes both alcohol and tobacco. Drugs and psychotropic substances are not going to go away as if by magic. 99

Reclassifying a drug

The decision to include or reclassify a drug in the ABC system is always met with further controversy. Growing expectation in 2006 that crystal meth was set to rise in popularity in the UK led many to argue it should be reclassified as a Class A drug, highlighting the harm caused by the amphetamine. However, concerns were raised the resulting publicity from reclassifying the drug would draw attention to its effects and inadvertently increase its use. Nevertheless, in January 2007, crystal meth was reclassified as a Class A drug.

The reclassification of cannabis has provoked similar controversy. In 2004 it was revised downwards from a Class B to a Class C drug after it was argued this would give police more time to concentrate on 'hard' drug users. In practice this means it is unlikely an adult caught in possession of cannabis will be arrested and charged. Instead they will likely receive a warning and have the drug confiscated, unless certain conditions apply.

14 November 2007

www.politics.co.uk

Mini glossary

prohibitive – *making something illegal*

intention – *purpose of plan*

abstinence – *choosing not to do something*

psychotropic – *a drug that affects the mind*

controversy – *a debate in which there is strong disagreement*

inadvertently – *without meaning to*

Q&A: cannabis reclassification

Why is cannabis in the news?

The Home Office has gone against the opinion of its own medical advisers by announcing that cannabis will be upgraded to class B again. The Advisory Council on the Misuse of Drugs published the findings of a review of the drug's classification, which concluded that cannabis should remain class C.

What did the review look at?

Gordon Brown ordered the review in response to concerns among doctors and MPs that the current classification of cannabis did not reflect the danger it poses to users' health. Several studies carried out since the drug was downgraded from class B in 2004 have warned that it damages users' mental health.

What are the health concerns?

There is particular concern about skunk, a strong form of cannabis linked to mental health disorders. In 2005, 10,000 11 to 17-year-olds were treated for cannabis use – 10 times the number a decade ago.

Cannabis plants are increasingly grown at home and include high levels of the active ingredient of cannabis, THC – delta-9-tetrahydrocannabinol – which encourages addiction and can cause symptoms including short-term memory loss and anxiety and panic attacks.

During their review of the drug's classification, the advisory council was told that the incidence of new schizophrenia cases reported to GPs had gone down, not up, between 1998 and 2005, indicating a weak link between increased strength and use in the past two decades and mental health problems.

Public views on cannabis

This poll attempts to gauge the level of public awareness concerning cannabis classification and assess opinions about its reclassification.

'As far as you understand, what is the current classification of cannabis?'

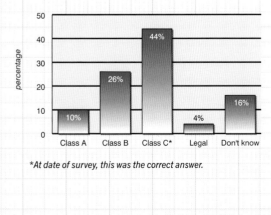

*At date of survey, this was the correct answer.

'And in what class or classification do you think cannabis should be in?'

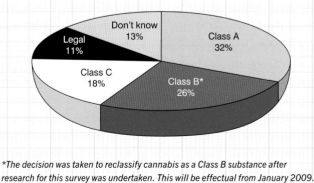

*The decision was taken to reclassify cannabis as a Class B substance after research for this survey was undertaken. This will be effectual from January 2009.

Source: Ipsos MORI, 'AMCD General Public Polling: Public views on cannabis', 5 February 2008. Results are based on 1,003 telephone interviews with adults aged 16+, conducted between 11 and 13 January 2008.

Q&A: cannabis reclassification

Are the mental health worries justified?

What is not clear from the research is whether the psychotic symptoms linked to cannabis use are only short-term or whether they may continue after use of the drug has stopped.

▶ In 2005, a Danish study found that almost half the patients treated for cannabis-related mental disorder went on to develop schizophrenia.

▶ The mental health charity Mind found the number of people taken to hospital with psychotic episodes had risen since cannabis was downgraded to class C.

▶ A summary of research into the effects of cannabis on psychosis published in the *Lancet* last year concluded that smoking cannabis increased the risk of schizophrenia by at least 40%.

▶ The advisory council was apparently persuaded to recommend keeping the drug's class C status after examining the findings of a new study by Keele University. The study found no evidence that rising cannabis use in the 1970s, 1980s and early 1990s had led to increases in the incidence of schizophrenia later on.

▶ Mental health campaigners point out that although the health risks are significant, reported use has also fallen since the classification of cannabis was downgraded. According to the British crime survey, 21.4% of 16-24-year-olds had used cannabis in 2005-06, compared with 28.2% in 1998-99.

> 66 *Several charities believe another change in the legal status of the drug is unnecessary.* 99

By David Batty, 7 May 2008

© Guardian Newspapers Limited 2008

How would reclassification affect cannabis users?

If cannabis were again made a class B drug, it would carry more severe penalties for possession. The maximum penalty for being found in possession of a class C drug is two years in prison plus an unlimited fine; for class B drugs it is five years in jail plus an unlimited fine.

The maximum penalty for supplying or dealing class C drugs and B drugs is the same - 14 years imprisonment plus an unlimited fine.

The Association of Chief Police Officers said it would not adopt a tougher approach towards the simple possession of cannabis if ministers upgraded the drug to class B again.

Who supports upgrading cannabis again?

Several mental health charities believe reclassification would raise awareness of the links between cannabis use and psychotic illness.

Sane, which gave evidence to the government review, said it knew of hundreds of cases where heavy users of cannabis, particularly skunk, went on to suffer psychotic breakdowns, hallucinations and paranoia.

Who else objects to reclassification?

Several charities believe another change in the legal status of the drug is unnecessary. The mental health charity Rethink said restoring the drug's class B status was a waste of time and money but it welcomed the government's commitment to a public health campaign.

Drug smuggling

ILLEGAL DRUGS CAN TOUCH THE LIVES of everyone. You might be affected directly if you have a friend or a family member who is a drug user, or indirectly through having to live with the threat of drug-related crime.

Experts estimate the worldwide illegal drugs trade is worth as much as the individual oil, gas or world tourism industries. Whatever the true figure, the UK alone spends more than one billion pounds tackling the problem.

Overseas threat

Illegal manufacture of heroin and cocaine is almost unheard of in the UK. Most of the drugs taken by British users come from thousands of miles away on different continents. They are shipped into our country by well-organised chains of international criminals.

▶ Much of the heroin sold in the UK comes from opium poppies grown in Afghanistan. It is processed and moved through 'route countries' such as Turkey, Iran, Pakistan and the Far East before being smuggled into Britain through Europe.

▶ Cocaine is similar but its origins are more likely to be South American. A great deal is routed through the Caribbean and Mexico, then travels through Spain, Portugal, France, Belgium and the Netherlands before making it into the hands of British dealers.

▶ Belgium and the Netherlands are major sources of synthetic drugs, such as ecstasy and amphetamine; although production of synthetic drugs appears to be on the rise in the UK, too.

▶ The main source countries for cannabis are Morocco, Russia, Pakistan, Lebanon, Columbia, Mexico, Jamaica and Nigeria.

Smugglers and their techniques

Traffickers try a huge variety of scams to get past our officers. We routinely seize drugs that have been:

▶ swallowed or stuffed by someone inside their body;

▶ hidden on a person;

▶ packed into someone's luggage or belongings;

▶ stashed in a car, boat or aeroplane;

▶ hidden in seemingly legal cargo.

The use of guns and violence

Some drugs gangs use the threat of extreme violence to protect their cargo. It's not just detection which threatens their shipments, but theft by rival criminals.

A kilo of heroin costs less than £1,000 in Pakistan but on British streets it is worth more than 75 times as much. This potential profit has drawn major organised crime syndicates to drug smuggling. But trafficking also carries massive risks, including some of the most severe international legal penalties.

This means that some drug traffickers are violent and carry guns. It means our officers – who are unarmed – have to work closely with armed police specialists to stop these potentially ruthless criminals.

Mini glossary

smuggling – bringing goods in or out of a country illegally

seize – take possession of

cargo – goods being transported

crime syndicates – criminal organisations

http://customs.hmrc.gov.uk

The above information is reprinted with kind permission from HM Revenue and Customs. © Crown copyright

Should drugs be legalised?

SOME PEOPLE ARGUE THAT the law should be changed and all drugs should be legalised or decriminalised. Some of the arguments for and against legalisation are outlined below.

 Many dangerous and lethal drugs are already legal. "

Arguments for legalising drugs

1. Government could regulate the quality of the drugs. This would prevent dangerous varieties of drugs being offered to unaware consumers.

2. It would reduce criminal activity. Organised criminals can make money from the trade in illegal drugs.

3. The government could collect tax revenue from the sale of drugs. It would also save the money spent on unsuccessfully trying to stop the illegal sale of drugs.

4. The government have been helping to reduce tobacco use over the past two decades, even though it is legal. Illegal drug use, however, has been continuing to grow.

Of course, many dangerous and lethal drugs are already legal.

► Tobacco is one of the UK's biggest killers. Between 1950 and 2000, 42 per cent of deaths in middle age (35-69) in UK men were caused by smoking, peaking in the 1960s when tobacco caused half of all deaths in middle-aged men.

► The number of alcohol related deaths in the UK has doubled in the past 20 years. In 2005, the number of deaths reached 8356.

The number of deaths from 'illegal drugs' is much smaller, although this is partly due to the fact less people take the drugs.

Arguments against legalising drugs

1. Making drugs legal would encourage people to use them. The current law discourages people from using drugs, whereas legalisation would make drugs more accessible and young people in particular may be more likely to experiment.

2. Drugs have serious health risks and many are also highly addictive. People still underestimate the dangers of illegal drugs and legalising them may send out the wrong message.

3. If drugs were legalised in the UK, drug addicts may be attracted to the UK. This is a strong argument against legalising drugs.

Mini glossary

consumers – *people who buy goods*

tax – *a charge placed on goods by the government*

tax revenue – *government income from taxes*

www.economicshelp.org

The above information is reprinted with kind permission from Economics Essays. © Economics Essays

Activities

Brainstorm

Brainstorm to find out what you know about tackling drugs.

1. What is the Misuse of Drugs Act?

   ....

   ....

2. What are the three classes of drugs and what penalties do they carry for possession and supply?

   ....

   ....

   ....

Oral activities

3. Tobacco and alcohol are legal drugs which are widely used in the UK, despite the fact that they can damage people's health. Do you think all drugs should be illegal? Discuss in a group.

   NOTES..

   ....

   ....

4. Read the article *Q&A: cannabis reclassification* on pages 22-23 and consider the arguments for and against reclassifying cannabis to a class B drug. Debate the issue with a partner, in which one of you argues for reclassification and the other against.

   NOTES..

   ....

Moral Dilemmas

5. Imagine you are a politician voting on whether all drugs should be legalised. Having considered both sides of the argument, how would you vote and why?

6. Imagine that one of your friends asks you to look after a small amount of cannabis for them, as they have already been in trouble with the police and they don't want to risk getting caught with drugs. Considering the possible consequences of being caught with drugs, what do you do?

Activities

Research activities

7. Do some research into where someone with a drug problem can go for help in your area. Do you think there is enough advice and support available for people with drug addictions?

    NOTES..
    ....
    ....
    ....
    ....

8. Research how a drug such as heroin or cocaine gets to the UK. What impact does drug trafficking have on the developing countries it is grown in?

    NOTES..
    ....
    ....
    ....
    ....

Written activities

Complete the following activities in your exercise books or on a sheet of paper.

9. Create a timeline charting the history of drug legislation in the UK. Use the article *Drug legislation* on page 19 as a starting point.

10. Read the article *Drugs and politics* on pages 20-21. Write your own drugs act listing the main points you think would reduce the harm caused by illegal drugs. Include your own classification system outlining the penalties you think different drugs should have.

Design activities

11. Design a poster to illustrate the possible consequences of being caught with drugs.
    The poster should be designed to discourage young people from experimenting with drugs.

Key Facts

- In the UK, the main piece of legislation covering drugs is the Misuse of Drugs Act first introduced in 1971. The act groups drugs into various classifications, using an A, B and C grouping where class A is considered the most harmful and therefore has the highest penalty. (page 2)

- Drugs are usually placed into three broad categories based upon their effects: stimulants, depressants and hallucinogens. (page 2)

- Cannabis is the most widely used illegal drug in Britain. (page 3)

- There have been over 200 ecstasy-related deaths since 1996. (page 5)

- It is estimated that each year in the UK around 114,000 people die from tobacco-related diseases. (page 9)

- In 2007, 17% of pupils aged 11 to 15 said they had taken drugs in the last year and 10% in the last month. The prevalence of drug use is similar among boys and girls, and increases with age. (page 10)

- Cannabis supply to young people is largely through social networks and friendship groups rather than through criminal drug markets. (page13)

- Over the last decade, use of illegal drugs in the UK has fallen to an 11-year low. Drug-related crime has dropped by a fifth over the last five years. (page 16)

- The Government is investing £604 million in drug treatment in 2008/09. (page 18)

- A study published in the Lancet in spring 2007 concluded UK drugs policy was not fit for purpose. Looking at the harm caused by various narcotic substances, it found alcohol was the fifth most dangerous drug available, following heroin, cocaine, barbiturates and methadone, yet it is not included in the ABC system. Tobacco emerged as the ninth most dangerous drug, ahead of cannabis and the Class A drugs ecstasy and LSD. (page 21)

- 32% of respondents surveyed by Ipsos MORI in January 2008 felt that cannabis should be classified as a Class A drug, the most harmful category for illegal substances. 26% felt it should be a Class B substance, while 18% of respondents were happy with the current Class C classification.11% thought it should be legal. (page 22)

- Experts estimate the worldwide illegal drugs trade is worth as much as the individual oil, gas or world tourism industries. (page 24)

Glossary

Addiction – A dependence on a substance which makes it very difficult to stop taking it.

AIDS – AIDS (acquired immune deficiency syndrome) is a disease caused by the virus HIV (human immunodeficiency virus). HIV weakens the body's immune system so that it can't fight infections.

Amphetamines – Man-made drugs which can be swallowed, inhaled or injected. Their effects can include increased mental alertness, energy and confidence.

Dealing – Supplying drugs to another person, usually in return for money. However, giving drugs away free to friends is also classed as dealing.

Dependence – Being reliant on something.

Depressant – A substance that slows down the nervous system, making the user feel calmer and more relaxed. Examples include alcohol, heroin and tranquillisers.

Drug – A chemical that alters the way the mind and body works. Legal drugs include alcohol, tobacco, caffeine and prescription medicines taken for medical reasons. Illegal drugs taken for recreation include cannabis, cocaine, ecstasy and speed.

Hallucinogen – A drug that causes hallucinations and produces visions and sensations which are removed from reality (a 'trip'), including LSD, ketamine and magic mushrooms.

Misuse of Drugs Act 1971 – Controls the use of dangerous recreational substances, making it an offence to possess banned drugs for personal use or with the intent to supply.

Opiate – Drugs made from the opium poppy, such as heroin, methadone and morphine.

Overdose – This occurs when an individual takes such a large dose of a drug that their body cannot cope with the effects, which can cause organ failure, coma and death.

Prohibition – A law that forbids something.

Psychosis – A severe mental disorder.

Reclassification – When an illegal substance is moved from one drugs class into another.

Schizophrenia – A mental illness marked by withdrawal from reality and hallucinations. There is some evidence of a link between cannabis use and schizophrenia.

Stimulant – A substance that speeds up the nervous system, making people feel more alert or energised. Examples include caffeine, cocaine, ecstasy and speed.

Solvent – A volatile substance which gives off fumes. Vapours from products including paint, glue and aerosols can be inhaled and cause intoxication.

Substance abuse – Substance abuse or misuse can refer to taking drugs or to being dependent on a drug, depending on someone's definition of 'misuse'.

Tolerance – The way in which the body becomes used to a drug when it is taken repeatedly. This means larger amounts of the drug are needed for it to have the same effect.

Trafficking – Trading illegal drugs.

Withdrawal – The symptoms that occur when a person stops taking a drug they are physically dependent on, causing flu-like symptoms.